Marijuana=

Laura S. Jeffrey

Enslow Publishers, Inc.
40 Industrial Road
Box 398
Berkeley Heights, NJ 07922
USA

http://www.enslow.com

Library of Congress Cataloging-in-Publication Data

Jeffrey, Laura S.
     Marijuana=Busted! / Laura S. Jeffrey.
        p. cm. — (Busted!)
     Includes bibliographical references and index.
     ISBN 0-7660-2796-1
      1. Marijuana abuse—Juvenile literature. 2. Marijuana—Juvenile literature.
     3. Teenagers—Drug use—Juvenile literature. I. Title. II. Series.
     HV5822.M3J44 2005
     613.8'35—dc22

                                                                    2005034877

Printed in the United States of America

10 9 8 7 6 5 4 3 2 1

To Our Readers:
We have done our best to make sure all Internet Addresses in this book were active and
appropriate when we went to press. However, the author and the publisher have no control
over and assume no liability for the material available on those Internet sites or on other Web
sites they may link to. Any comments or suggestions can be sent by e-mail to
comments@enslow.com or to the address on the back cover.

Illustration Credits: Associated Press, pp. 8, 18–19, 25, 40, 48, 73, 82; BananaStock,
pp. 34, 46, 68; Digital Stock, pp. 10, 53, 62–63; Courtesy of the Drug Enforcement
Administration, pp. 14, 42; © 2006 Jupiterimages, pp. 30–31, 50–51, 85; Courtesy of the
National Institute on Drug Abuse, p. 22; photodisc, pp. 4–5; stockbyte, pp. 58, 78–79.

Cover Illustration: Associated Press.

CONTENTS

CHAPTER ONE

SHOTS IN THE NIGHT

Bang! Bang! Bang! Bang! Bang! Bang! Bang! Bang! Bang! Nine shots shattered the silence in a Virginia community. A visitor in the neighborhood that night said the noise sounded like a pipe hitting the pavement.[1] It was March 5, 2001. Prince William County police officers were called. When they arrived at the scene, they found the body of Daniel Petrole, Jr. The twenty-one-year-old had been shot dead while sitting in his car. The car was parked in the driveway of Petrole's townhouse. Witnesses reported seeing a red car speed away from the neighborhood.

At first, police thought Petrole might have been the victim of "road rage." Perhaps Petrole had been out driving around, and had become involved in an incident with another driver. The other driver might have followed Petrole home and then shot him.

Clues quickly pointed police in another direction. Petrole had almost one thousand dollars in his pocket. Almost twenty thousand dollars more was found in a duffel bag in his trunk.[2] Police found hundreds of thousands of dollars more in Petrole's house. The money was in a garbage bag stuffed under a bathroom sink.

Police also discovered ecstasy pills, and more than fifty pounds of marijuana. Police later learned that the marijuana was a very powerful variety. Regular street marijuana, also known as "schwag" or "swag," usually sells for about one thousand dollars a pound. This marijuana, nicknamed "chronic" or "kind bud," sells for five times that amount. Petrole was a drug dealer. His illegal occupation had proven to be deadly.

Petrole "should have expected what he got, and no one should be surprised by it," said another drug dealer. "He lived hard and fast and died young. A drug dealer died. That's what drug dealers do: They get killed or they go to jail."[3]

Yet Petrole seemed an unlikely drug dealer. His father was a retired Secret Service agent who had protected two United States presidents. His mother was a teacher. Petrole played on a travel soccer team in high school and attended church. He had a girlfriend and was taking classes at a community college.[4]

Petrole "was always respectful, always cooperative and seemed to get along with his peers," said one of his high school teachers.[5] A friend of the family described Petrole as "fun-loving, but not into anything that would be considered dangerous or stupid or illegal."[6]

Sadly, the friend was wrong. Sometime during his childhood, Petrole became involved with drugs. He started using marijuana, then he turned to selling it. Petrole hooked up with suppliers.

A Drug Enforcement Administration agent gives a freshly pulled marijuana plant to another law-enforcement officer in a national forest near Entiant, Washington.

First, he used one in Texas. Then, he found a supplier in Seattle, Washington.[7]

The supplier had access to very potent marijuana. Every month, he sent about one hundred pounds of marijuana to Petrole. Petrole divided it up, and then sold it at a higher price to other dealers. Those dealers marked up the price again, and sold it to their customers. Many of the customers were high school students.

Petrole did not require the dealers to pay him

right away. The dealers paid Petrole after they sold the marijuana to their customers.

As police learned more about Petrole's illegal occupation, they found evidence that led to his killer. In many ways, the killer was similar to the victim. Owen Barber was twenty-one years old. He was from a middle-class family. He also was a drug user, and a drug dealer. Barber was arrested and confessed to the crime.

Barber told police that he helped his friend, Justin Wolfe, sell marijuana. Wolfe received marijuana from Petrole. Then, Wolfe and Barber sold it to others. Wolfe owed Petrole a lot of money— almost seventy thousand dollars. Barber told police that Wolfe paid him to kill Petrole. Wolfe had no trouble selling the marijuana, but he did not want to pay his drug debt. Barber said Wolfe decided it would be better to kill Petrole rather than pay him the money he owed.[8]

The night he died, Petrole drove to Wolfe's house to deliver some marijuana. Barber was waiting in his car and followed Petrole home. When Petrole parked his car, Barber pulled up to it. "I got out of my car and shot him through the passenger window," Barber said. "I shot a full clip,

Involvement in any sort of drug-related activity will most likely end the same way—jail time.

from about three, four or five feet away. . . . He had to be dead . . . all those bullets, that close."[9]

"We slid him out of the car, and all the blood came out of [his] side," said a friend of Petrole's roommate, who had heard the gunshots. "I knew he was dead when I found him."[10]

Barber pleaded guilty to first-degree murder and was sentenced to thirty-eight years in prison. Wolfe also was arrested. He was charged with hiring Barber to commit murder. Wolfe pleaded not guilty. He said he had nothing to do with Petrole's death. During Wolfe's trial, Barber testified against his old friend.

The jury believed Barber. Wolfe was convicted of murder. Wolfe begged the jurors not to recommend a death sentence. "I don't want to die. I don't want the death penalty," he said.[11] But the jurors believed death to be the proper punishment. Wolfe was sentenced to death. He was twenty years old. Today, Wolfe is believed to be the youngest person on Virginia's death row.

Wolfe could have had a successful life. Petrole and Barber could have, too. Instead, they all chose the same, wrong path. As Wolfe said, "I know that if I hadn't been involved in selling marijuana, I wouldn't be here [in prison]."[12]

The police not only solved a murder, but they also broke up a huge drug ring. Shortly after Petrole's death, Prince William County police contacted the Drug Enforcement Administration (DEA). The DEA enforces the nation's drug laws, and helps bring criminals to justice. The DEA is a federal agency. It joins local investigations that involve large quantities of drugs and a lot of people.[13]

DEA agents worked with Prince William County police officers. They interviewed drug dealers and their customers. Those interviews led to people in other states including Texas, Washington, Michigan, and Florida. "People talk, and from there it goes," said Kevin Foley, assistant special agent in charge of the DEA's Washington, D.C., division.[14] In all, police officers and DEA agents talked to almost fifty people connected to the drug ring itself.

The officers and DEA agents also examined phone records, credit card receipts, and other financial information.

"Petrole was involved in a conspiracy. It

involved people who sold him drugs, and people he sold drugs to," said Steve Straka, a retired special agent with the Virginia State Police. Straka had been assigned to a DEA task force.

"When we investigated Petrole's murder, we identified people that were associated with him who had their own little conspiracy going on with other people—maybe other suppliers and other customers," Straka said. "So in the end, we not only arrested people that [Petrole] was selling to and dealing with, but other people involved in the distribution of marijuana and ecstasy."[15]

Many of the drug dealers were men who had graduated from high school only a few years earlier. They knew what they were doing was illegal, but they did not realize how dangerous it was.

"Now they know it is anything but harmless," said the prosecutor of the case, Richard Conway. Another prosecutor, Paul Ebert said, "They see what it can lead to. It has changed a lot of lifestyles, and it has definitely caused a change in attitude."[16]

Marijuana has many slang terms, including hashish or hash, pot, grass, herb, weed, reefer, ganja, and Mary Jane. These terms have been around for many, many years. More recently, some communities in the United States have developed their own nicknames for marijuana. These include chronic, schwag, swag, and skunk.

Marijuana, no matter what a person calls it, is

Marijuana, by any name, is a dangerous and illegal drug.

Street Names for Marijuana

Blunt	Mary Jane
Doobie	Pot
Dope	Reefer
Ganja or Ganga	Roach
Grass	Skunkweed
Herb	Wacky weed
Joint	Weed

a dangerous and illegal drug. It is also the most commonly used illegal drug in the United States.[17] Millions of Americans have tried marijuana. Former presidents and presidential candidates, soldiers, students, musicians, and talk show hosts are among those who admit they have tried it or use it.

According to recent statistics, more than six million American adults have a marijuana habit. Additionally, three million adults are dependent on marijuana.[18] Being dependent means that people continue to use marijuana even though they realize the drug has caused them great physical and emotional damage.

Why have so many people tried marijuana?

Why do so many people continue to use it? Experts believe it is because there are so many misconceptions about the drug. Many people think marijuana is harmless—after all, it is a plant. But marijuana is not harmless. Many people think marijuana is not addictive. But marijuana is addictive. Many people think marijuana does not adversely affect driving, athletic performance, or

How Do You Know if Someone is Using Marijuana?

It might be hard to tell, but the following are some warning signs:

- Dizziness and trouble walking
- Red, bloodshot eyes
- Clothes and hair smell like smoke
- Difficulty remembering things that just happened
- Acting silly for no reason

Help someone who is using marijuana or other drugs by being a true friend. Encourage the person to talk to a trusted adult.

concentration. But marijuana does adversely affect all those things.

There are many myths about marijuana. There are also many important facts. Here are two of them: Marijuana is dangerous, and marijuana is illegal. As the lives of Petrole, Wolfe, and Barber prove, not knowing those two facts can lead to a dead-end future.

CHAPTER TWO

A POWERFUL PLANT

Thanks to strong police work, Daniel Petrole's drug ring was destroyed and several drug dealers were arrested. They were convicted of their crimes and sentenced to many, many years in prison.

Unfortunately, however, marijuana remains available on Virginia's streets.

In the fall of 2005, more than four years after Petrole's murder, Officer Angela Hanby was called to Marsteller Middle School. The school is located in the same county where Petrole lived.

Hanby was called to the school by Marsteller's security officer, who had received a tip from a student. The student said another student, Adam (not his real name), had brought marijuana to school.

The security officer questioned Adam. At first, Adam denied having marijuana. The officer asked him what he had in his pocket. Adam said he had only money. But when Adam pulled out the money to show it to the officer, a small, plastic bag fell out of his pocket. The plastic bag contained a dark, dry, shredded mixture.

As soon as Hanby arrived at the school, the security officer showed her the bag. Following procedure, Hanby took it and later sent it to a state laboratory for testing. But by looking at and smelling the substance, Hanby knew right away: The bag contained marijuana.[1]

Marijuana comes from the *cannabis sativa* plant. The drug is made from the plant's dried flowers, stems, seeds, and leaves. This shredded mixture is brown, green, or gray in color. Marijuana has a sharp, unique odor. It smells sweet and sour at the same time. When marijuana is burned, the smell is even stronger.

Marijuana contains almost four hundred chemicals. The main chemical is delta-9-tetrahydrocannabinol, or THC. When a person uses marijuana, the THC travels through the bloodstream to the brain and other organs in the body.

In the brain, THC latches on to places on the nerve cells called cannabinoid receptors. The THC overstimulates these receptors. The overstimulation of the pleasure receptors causes users to feel "high." Other receptors affect memory, thought, concentration, perceptions of time, and coordination.[2] The THC overstimulates these receptors, too.

Smoking marijuana enables the THC to travel quickly through the bloodstream to the brain. The slang terms for marijuana cigarettes are joints

Did You Know...

Most teens are not using marijuana. According to a 2002 study, about four out of five 12- to 17-year-olds had never tried marijuana.

and nails. Users take special paper and sprinkle the marijuana onto the middle of it. Then, they roll up the paper, light the end, and smoke. Marijuana also can be smoked in a special pipe called a bong.

Some marijuana smokers take the tobacco out of a regular cigar. Then, they refill the cigar with marijuana. The slang term for this type of cigar is

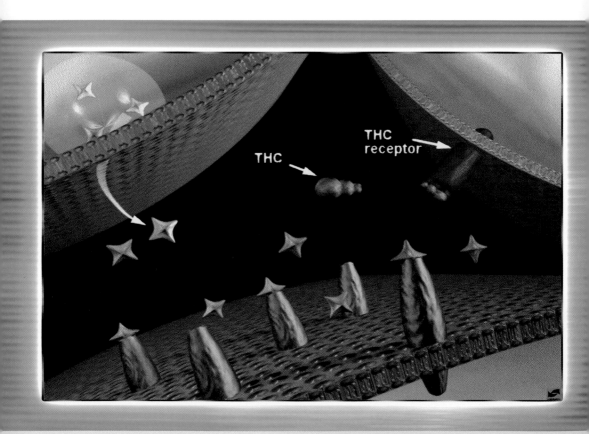

THC causes the release of dopamine in the brain, which causes the user to feel "high."

a blunt. The marijuana in a blunt may be mixed with or dipped into other illegal drugs.

Some users eat marijuana by baking it into foods. Or, they drink marijuana by brewing it as a tea. It takes longer for the THC to reach the brain when the marijuana is eaten or drunk. When marijuana is smoked, the THC gets to the brain within minutes. When marijuana is eaten or drunk, it takes up to three hours to reach the brain.[3]

Through smoking marijuana, THC reaches the brain quickly. However, THC does not easily dissolve in blood. So while some THC reaches the brain, the rest collects in body fat. Then, the THC slowly and steadily is released throughout the body. After a while, users may no longer feel the effects of marijuana. However, the THC remains in the body for several days, or even several weeks.

The THC "gets stored in the body fat and released," said Eric Zehr, vice president of addiction and behavioral services at the Illinois Institute for Addiction Recovery. "It varies by the person and by the amount of body fat, but someone may be under the influence and not even realize it for up to thirty days."[4]

The more often a person uses marijuana, the more THC is stored in body fat. Drug tests can detect marijuana in a user's urine several days after that person has last used the drug. With heavy users, drug tests can detect marijuana several weeks after the last use.[5]

Teresa S. Latham is a counselor in the Student Assistance Program for Fairfax County's Alcohol and Drug Youth Services in Virginia. She divides her time among three high schools and two middle schools. Students who are caught with marijuana on school property are sent to Latham for an assessment. An assessment determines if the student needs drug treatment. Parents, teachers, and school administrators can also request assessments of students. Latham uses a separate office that is not on school property to conduct the assessments.

Part of the assessment is giving a drug test. Latham says these drug tests are observed tests. This mean someone watches the student while the student gives a urine sample. The test is observed to make sure the student does not try to use someone else's urine, or water down his or her own sample.

A lab technician tests urine samples for THC and other drugs.

To complete the drug test, the student takes a sample cup into the bathroom. The student is accompanied by an adult. If a male student is taking the test, a man observes the test. If it is a female student, a woman observes the test.

The student urinates into the small, plastic cup, which has been labeled with his or her name. Then, the student gives the cup to the adult. The adult seals the cup and places it in a sterile bag. The bag also is labeled with the student's name. The sample is placed in a refrigerator and locked. About once a week, a driver arrives to pick up the samples. The driver takes the samples to the Fairfax County Health Department. The samples are tested in the laboratory there for THC.[6]

Laboratory technicians test the substance to determine if it contains THC. If there is any amount of THC, then the substance is marijuana. For court proceedings, any amount of THC is illegal.

Usually, laboratory technicians do not conduct tests to figure out how much THC the marijuana contains and thus, how strong it is. However, DEA laboratory technicians sometimes do soil analysis and other tests to determine in what part of the world the marijuana was grown.[7]

When police officers make drug arrests, they sometimes use field kits to determine whether the substance they find on a suspect is marijuana. But to press charges, they must obtain an official test result from a state laboratory. This test result will be used in court.

Some drug dealers mix marijuana with other illegal drugs, such as PCP, also known as angel dust. Others try to fool buyers. They put grass clippings or oregano, an Italian spice, in a bag, and then they sell it as marijuana to their customers. Even though the substance is not actually an illegal drug, the seller can get in as much trouble as if it were marijuana.

There are many different varieties of the *cannabis sativa* plant. One type is nicknamed

Did You Know ...

THC, the active ingredient in marijuana, affects the nerve cells in the part of the brain where memories are formed.

"skunk weed." It is called this because it smells like a skunk when it is burned.[8]

Over the years, growers have experimented to produce plants with higher and higher levels of THC. The more THC that is in the marijuana, the more powerful it is. Some experts estimate that today, THC levels in marijuana are more than fifty percent higher than they were about ten years ago.[9] Regular street marijuana, also known as swag, contains about 5 percent THC. More powerful marijuana, such as chronic, can contain more than 20 percent THC.[10] Some have even higher levels of THC.

Hemp is a type of *cannabis sativa* plant with an extremely low level of THC. Most experts believe there is not enough THC in hemp to lead to a "high." Historically, hemp has been used to make clothing, paper, building materials, paint, automobile parts, and other products.

It is Not Always What It Seems

Marijuana can be laced with other dangerous drugs or chemicals without the user's knowledge. It could be laced with crack cocaine, PCP, or even embalming fluid.

Most of the marijuana in the United States is brought into the country from Mexico. Canada also is one of the major suppliers of marijuana. Some people in the United States grow their own cannabis plants, to illegally sell to others or for their own use.

Today, it is illegal in the United States to grow any kind of *cannabis sativa,* even hemp. Several other countries have also outlawed it. But the *cannabis sativa* plant was not always considered off limits.

CHAPTER THREE

AN ANCIENT CROP

Cannabis sativa is a very old plant. It has grown around the world for thousands of years. As early as 2700 B.C., the Chinese grew cannabis. They used it to make rope, cloth, and paper. The Greeks and Romans used cannabis to make these items and medicine, too.

People in India also grew cannabis to

make medicine. Though there was no proof that it worked, the medicine was used to treat serious diseases, such as tuberculosis. Tuberculosis is a disease of the lungs. Cannabis also was used for common ailments such as dandruff, headaches, and toothaches.[1]

During the Middle Ages (A.D. 476 to 1450), Europeans planted hemp. So did the Pilgrims, who arrived in America in the early 1600s. The Pilgrims used hemp seeds for bartering with the American Indians. Bartering is trading goods or services instead of using money. Sometimes, hemp seeds substituted for money to pay taxes. Cannabis was so important to Virginia's economy that farmers in that colony were fined if they did

Trends in Lifetime Prevalence Use of Marijuana for Eighth, Tenth, and Twelfth Graders					
	2001	2002	2003	2004	2005
8th Grade	20.4	19.2	17.5	16.3	16.5
10th Grade	40.1	38.7	36.4	35.1	34.1
12th Grade	49.0	47.8	46.1	45.7	44.8

Source: Monitoring the Future

not grow it. During the Revolutionary War (1775–1783), when the United States fought Great Britain for independence, General George Washington and his soldiers wore uniforms made from hemp.

Cannabis was used for practical reasons. It also was used for pleasure. This is called recreational use. By the 1800s, New York and many other big cities had public smoking parlors. These smoking parlors were similar to today's restaurants and bars. Instead of ordering food or drink, people smoked hashish. Hashish is a stronger form of marijuana.

Many people believed cannabis was harmless. However, some people did not. In 1868, Egypt outlawed smoking or eating cannabis. Lawmakers in that country said using the drug caused people to become lazy.[2]

William Randolph Hearst (1863–1951) was an advocate against cannabis. Hearst was a very wealthy businessman in California. He owned several newspapers and magazines, among other companies. Hearst practiced what is called "yellow journalism." The term refers to publishing newspaper stories, illustrations, or photographs

Smoking marijuana could cause a person to be lazy and apathetic.

that are greatly exaggerated or totally false. Hearst and other newspaper publishers did this to attract readers and influence their opinions.

In the late 1800s, Hearst had lost thousands of acres of timberland to Mexican rebel Pancho Villa and his soldiers. Hearst was very angry because he used the trees on that land to manufacture newsprint, a type of paper. At the time, cannabis grew freely in Mexico, and many people there used it recreationally. Pancho Villa and his soldiers smoked marijuana. Hearst used his newspapers to get revenge. He published stories saying that all Mexicans were violent because they smoked marijuana.

Other stories in Hearst's newspapers said smoking marijuana led people to commit rapes and murders. Marijuana is, indeed, a harmful drug. However, very few experts believed it led people to commit such violent crimes. Hearst is credited with making the word "marijuana" a common term in the United States.[3]

In 1914, Congress passed the Harrison Act. This law made it a crime to use certain drugs unless they were prescribed by a doctor. The new law was passed to prevent recreational use of opium, morphine, and cocaine. Marijuana was not included, so recreational use continued to be legal. During the next several years, however, some states outlawed marijuana use. From 1915 to 1937, about 27 states passed laws against marijuana.[4]

In 1919, the United States Congress passed the 18th amendment to the Constitution. This amendment, also known as the Volstead Act, banned the manufacture or sale of any beverage that contained more than a tiny portion of alcohol. The law officially took effect in January 1920.

Many states had already outlawed alcohol, but with the passage of the 18th amendment, alcohol was illegal everywhere in the United States. This period in United States history is called Prohibition.

Alcohol was now against the law, so some people turned to marijuana. For example, many jazz musicians in New York City and New Orleans, Louisiana, used marijuana. They believed the drug

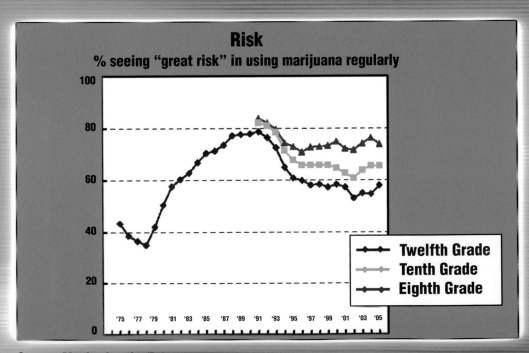

Risk

% seeing "great risk" in using marijuana regularly

Twelfth Grade
Tenth Grade
Eighth Grade

Source: Monitoring the Future

helped their sense of hearing, and enabled them to perform better. Several jazz songs written during this time period paid tribute to the drug.[5]

In 1930, the United States government established the Federal Bureau of Narcotics (FBN). This agency is now known as the Drug Enforcement Administration. Harry Anslinger was appointed by President Herbert Hoover to lead the FBN. Anslinger believed marijuana was a dangerous drug. He wanted it outlawed.

Years later, in 1933, Congress repealed the 18th amendment. To repeal means to officially cancel. Prohibition was over; alcohol was legal again. Yet marijuana remained popular. Anslinger continued to push for a ban against the drug.

Finally, in 1937, Congress passed the Marihuana Tax Act. (At the time, "marihuana" was the popular spelling of the drug.) The law required anyone who grew or possessed cannabis to pay taxes on it by purchasing a special government stamp, but the government did not print or sell any stamps. Anyone caught breaking the law would be prosecuted for tax evasion. In effect, the Marihuana Tax Act made using or possessing the drug illegal.

The Marihuana Tax Act applied to all cannabis plants, even those grown for practical reasons. Cannabis could no longer be legally grown in the United States to produce rope, cloth, or other products. By now, most of the cannabis, or hemp, used for these products was grown in the Far East and then imported to the United States.

During World War II (1941–1945), the Japanese seized many cannabis crops in the Far East. American manufacturers were unable to get the hemp they needed. The United States government provided hemp seeds to farmers. The farmers grew hemp for manufacturers to produce rope and other needed items for American

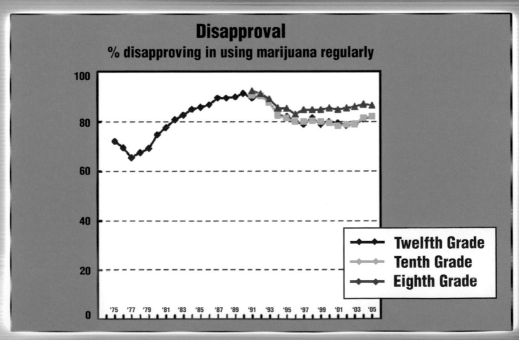

Disapproval
% disapproving in using marijuana regularly

Twelfth Grade
Tenth Grade
Eighth Grade

Source: Monitoring the Future

military forces.[6] The federal government also
established an official cannabis crop at the
University of Mississippi. Today, cannabis continues
to be grown there. The plants are used for
research.[7]

After World War II ended in 1945, the United
States and several countries joined together to
form the United Nations (U.N.) The international
organization's goals were to promote world
peace, work together to solve the world's problems, and encourage respect for human rights.

In the years that followed, the U.N. approved
several international treaties about the illegal
manufacturing and selling of drugs. A treaty is a
formal agreement between two or more nations.
The U.N. approved treaties for drugs including
opium, cocaine, and heroin.

These international treaties were combined
into one treaty in 1961. It was called the United
Nations Single Convention on Narcotic Drugs.
This treaty was expanded to include cannabis.
Medical experts believed marijuana to be harm-
ful. They also were fearful that marijuana would
lead users to try other, even more harmful drugs.
The treaty stated that using cannabis "for other

In 1961, the United Nations approved the United Nations Single Convention on Narcotic Drugs, which dealt with the illegal manufacturing and selling of drugs, including marijuana.

than medical and scientific purposes must be discontinued as soon as possible."[8]

Despite this treaty, people continued to use marijuana recreationally. Many American servicemen tried the drug when they served overseas during the Vietnam War (1959–1973). Young people in the United States also experimented with it. For example, a well-known United States senator and Vietnam veteran has admitted that he tried marijuana when he was a young man. "I didn't like it," he said. "I have never used or tried any drug since."[9]

In 1970, United States lawmakers passed the Controlled Substances Act. This law placed drugs into categories, or schedules. The schedules defined drugs by their potential to help people, and also by their potential to harm people. Schedule I drugs are the most dangerous drugs that also have the least medical value. Examples of Schedule I drugs are heroin, ecstasy, and LSD. Schedule V drugs are harmless drugs but with medical value, such as antibiotics. In 1970, marijuana was classified as a Schedule I drug.

In 1975, the University of Michigan's Institute for Social Research began surveying high school seniors about their drug use. The survey, called "Monitoring the Future," is conducted every year. It is paid for by the National Institute on Drug Abuse, the National Institutes of Health, and the Department of Health and Human Services. The survey of 1979 found that approximately 60 percent of all high school seniors said they had tried marijuana at least one time. Approximately 10 percent said they had used it daily for the past month.[10]

In 1980, former California Governor Ronald Reagan was elected president of the United States. During the presidential campaign, his wife, Nancy, visited a drug abuse treatment center in New York. After her husband became president, Mrs. Reagan adopted drug-abuse awareness as a cause. Her "Just Say No" campaign became very popular.

At the same time, interest in marijuana as a medicine grew. In the early 1980s, the National Cancer Institute asked the Drug Enforcement Administration to support studies on a pill called Marinol. Like marijuana, the main ingredient in Marinol is THC. The THC in Marinol is synthetic, which means it was not naturally produced.

The studies showed that Marinol helped relieve the nausea, vomiting, and pain that cancer patients experienced when they had

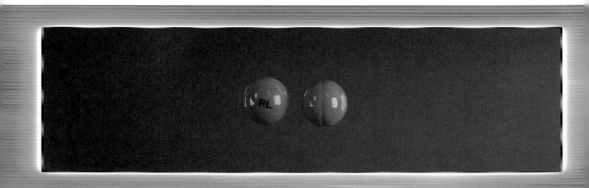

Marinol is synthetic THC in pill form. It has helped cancer patients as well as AIDS patients.

chemotherapy. Marinol also helped people with acquired immune deficiency syndrome (AIDS). AIDS patients often lose dangerous amounts of weight. Marinol helped increase the patients' appetite. Doctors began prescribing Marinol to very sick people.

In the late 1980s, President Reagan approved the creation of a new Office of National Drug Control Policy. William Bennett was named director of the agency.

The "Monitoring the Future" survey expanded in 1991 to include students in the eighth and tenth grades. Three years later, the survey found that almost 17 percent of eighth graders said they had used marijuana at least one time. Among tenth grade students, approximately 30 percent said they had tried marijuana at least one time. Approximately 38 percent of high school seniors said they had tried marijuana at least once.[11]

In 1996, voters in California passed Proposition 215. This bill, also know as the Compassionate Use Act, allowed doctors to prescribe marijuana to patients. The main purpose was for very ill and dying patients to legally use marijuana to ease their pain. With a doctor's permission, sick people could grow marijuana for their own use. They also could buy it from someone else. Private clubs were established to distribute marijuana to these sick people. Eventually, nine other states also passed laws allowing the use of "medical marijuana."

Barry McCaffrey, a retired Army general, became the fourth director of the Office of National Drug Control Policy in 1997. The next year, McCaffrey asked experts at the Institute of Medicine to study marijuana's usefulness as a medicine.

That study was released to the public in March 1999. It found that indeed, marijuana was beneficial for some patients with cancer or AIDS. Marinol helped these people manage pain and gain weight.

The study also found that smoking marijuana was not a good way for patients to receive the benefits of THC. In fact, smoking itself was dangerous. The hundreds of chemicals in marijuana would cause more harm to people who already were very ill. The study urged smoke-free methods of prescribing marijuana to sick people.[12]

Besides Marinol, another idea was to invent a "pot patch" for a person's arm.

"Marijuana shows encouraging results in some areas like pain management and nausea," said Igor Grant, director of the University of California's Center for Medical Cannabis Research. "But there is little evidence to suggest it has any benefit beyond a few defined areas."[13]

Further, the Medical Board of California said doctors should not recommend marijuana as a treatment for children except in extreme cases, and only with careful doctor supervision.[14]

On May 14, 2001, the United States Supreme Court ruled against states with medical marijuana laws. The nation's highest court said distributors of medical marijuana could be prosecuted under federal anti-drug charges. Two months later, the American Medical Association said marijuana should remain a Schedule I drug until more research could be done on its medical uses.

Two years later, the "Monitoring the Future" survey found that 17.5 percent of eighth graders said they had tried marijuana at least once. Approximately 36 percent of tenth graders, and 46 percent of high school seniors, also said they had tried the drug at least once. All of these percentages were increases from the 1994 survey.

In June 2005, the United States Supreme Court again ruled against medical marijuana. This ruling was a response to a lawsuit filed by Angel McClary Raich and Diane Monson. Raich and Monson were two very sick women in California. They used marijuana to ease their pain.

Two people who grew marijuana for Raich and Monson also were part of the lawsuit. These four

A recent survey found that approximately 36 percent of tenth graders and 46 percent of twelfth graders had tried marijuana at least once.

people wanted very ill Americans to have the legal right to grow and use marijuana for their own use. They also wanted the right to obtain marijuana from someone else, if necessary. The Supreme Court said states could not legalize marijuana for medical use.

Medical use remains controversial. In October 2005, singer Melissa Etheridge publicly announced that she had smoked marijuana during treatment for breast cancer. She said her doctors had recommended it. Talk show host Montel Williams, who was diagnosed with multiple sclerosis, has also said that he smokes marijuana for medical reasons.

Just as there is controversy about medical marijuana, there also is controversy about punishing people who are caught using or possessing marijuana. Almost everyone agrees there should be harsh penalties for people who sell marijuana, particularly for those who sell it to children. But some states say punishment should be light for adults who use marijuana recreationally. As of 2004, eleven states had decriminalized marijuana. Decriminalize means to reduce or eliminate legal penalties.

Not all states agree, however. In 2004, Nevada citizens voted against a proposal that would make it legal for adults to have a small amount of marijuana. "People are sympathetic to medical marijuana," said one person. "But if the marijuana is used as a recreational drug to intoxicate there is no groundswell of support."[15]

Marijuana use is an issue in other countries as well. Canada and England are among countries that have decriminalized the drug. Adults who

Talk show host Montel Williams has said he smokes marijuana as a medical treatment for multiple sclerosis.

have small amounts for their personal use will not be punished harshly if they are caught.

Even those who want to decriminalize marijuana make it clear that they do not think children should use it. For example, Eric Schlosser is an award-winning journalist who believes marijuana use should be decriminalized for adults. Schlosser wrote an article for *The New York Times* criticizing the United States government's war on marijuana. In the article, Schlosser wrote that marijuana "is a powerful, mind-altering drug. It should not be smoked by young people."[16]

Many people believe it is a big mistake to decriminalize marijuana. The British Medical Association, for example, expressed "extreme concern" about it. This group of doctors worried that decriminalizing marijuana might lead people to believe marijuana is safe to use.[17] As doctors, they know all too well: It is not.

CHAPTER FOUR

CHANGE IN THE BRAIN

Ryan Shafer was in the sixth grade when he first tried marijuana. He quickly became a heavy user. By the time Ryan was a teenager, he was a drug addict. He used marijuana along with several other illegal drugs, including LSD and ecstasy. Ryan was failing school when his parents finally became aware of his problem. They tried desperately to help him. They sent him to drug-treatment programs. Ryan did better, for awhile. But he always returned to his destructive ways.

One night, when he was sixteen years old, Ryan drove to the house of a drug dealer. On the way back to his own home, he was in a minor car accident. Ryan got out of his car and started running. A car hit him. The driver of that car tried to help him. But Ryan kept running. He ran onto a highway. A van hit him head-on and killed him.[1]

"It was marijuana that started Ryan on his downfall," his father said. Marijuana "was always the drug he went back to."[2]

Marijuana did not lead to the death of Jeb (not his real name). But it did play a role in him accidentally killing someone else. The seventeen-year-old, who lives in Indiana, was "stoned," or high on marijuana, one night. He climbed onto a highway overpass. There, he found a concrete block and tipped it off the overpass. At that moment, a car drove by. The concrete block crashed through the passenger front window of the car. Jose Hernandez, a husband and father, was killed instantly. Hernandez's wife and four

Drivers who are "stoned" react differently than drivers who are drunk. Both conditions are dangerous and unsafe because the drivers are impaired.

children were also in the car. They witnessed the horrible accident.[3]

Many people believe marijuana is a harmless drug. But as scientists have conducted more studies, they have learned how dangerous it is. Marijuana is a mind-altering drug. The main chemical, THC, changes how the brain works. These changes can be short-term, or temporary. But they also can be long-term, or permanent. Some studies have found that regular use of marijuana leads to brain changes that are similar to the changes caused by cocaine, heroin, and alcohol.[4]

Theresa Latham, a school counselor, said she is amazed at how many students think marijuana is harmless. "They say, 'It's natural, it's grows from the ground. It's a plant,'" she said. "I tell them, "So is arsenic," a very poisonous and deadly substance. "So is poison ivy, but you wouldn't want to rub it on your face."[5]

Marijuana affects people differently. Those reactions depend on how much marijuana a person uses, and the amount of the THC in the marijuana. Reactions also depend on whether the person has used marijuana in the past, and if alcohol and other drugs are also being used at the same time.

Users who smoke marijuana can feel changes within a few minutes. They feel a sense of pleasure, or a "high." Also, their mouths become dry. Their eyes become red because the blood vessels expand. They lose coordination and balance. They take longer to react. They also have trouble remembering details. They may lose sense of what time it is. Sometimes, blood pressure increases and the heart beats faster. After a few hours, the immediate effects of marijuana fade. The user then may become very sleepy.

The short-term effects of marijuana are temporary. However, these short-term effects can have lasting consequences. For example, one study found that marijuana users showed the same lack of coordination as drunk drivers.[6]

Drivers who are "stoned" react differently than drivers who are drunk. A driver under the influence of marijuana might drive too slowly, while a drunken driver might drive too fast. Both conditions are unsafe because the drivers are impaired. Marijuana may lead a driver to lose focus or become disoriented. A driver high on marijuana may even fall asleep at the wheel. Drivers who have used both alcohol and marijuana are especially dangerous.

"Driving under the influence of marijuana is no better or safer than driving under the influence of alcohol," said Latham. "Many teens have a total lack of understanding about this. You cannot and should not drive under the influence of anything."[7]

In another study, pilots were given marijuana. Twenty hours later, the pilots were tested in their ability to operate flight simulators. The pilots did not have the coordination or mental ability to properly operate the simulators. Additionally, the pilots were not aware that they were disabled. They reported that they no longer felt the effects of the marijuana they had used almost a day before.[8]

The THC in marijuana also inhibits nausea. This is beneficial for cancer patients, who often vomit excessively because of chemotherapy treatments. But it could prove deadly to marijuana users who also consume too much alcohol.[9] They might die because they are unable to vomit to rid their body of the poisonous substance.

Long term, marijuana can cause brain damage. Researchers are studying the possibility that regular marijuana use may change the brain so that users are more likely to become addicted to cocaine and other drugs.[10]

Another study found that people who smoked marijuana had changes in the flow of blood to their brain. This blood-flow change explains why marijuana users have trouble thinking and remembering. The study found that in some marijuana users, the blood-flow levels did not improve, even after they stopped using the drug.[11]

People who begin using marijuana at an early age may be more likely to develop mental health disorders, such as depression, suicidal thoughts, and schizophrenia. Researchers are not sure if marijuana causes the disorders, or if people who are more likely to develop the disorders are also more likely to use marijuana.

Dr. Robert Heath of Tulane Medical School researched the effects of marijuana on the brains of monkeys. He found that after two months of smoking, serious damage had occurred. The damage was particularly severe in the part of the brain that controls emotions.[12]

Marijuana is particularly harmful for young people because their brains have not yet fully developed. Studies have shown that the younger a person is when he or she starts using marijuana, the greater the risk that the person will develop problems because of marijuana use. If there is a history of substance abuse in that young person's family, the risk of problems is even higher.[13]

Marijuana damages more than the brain. It also damages the lungs. One marijuana cigarette contains as much as four times the tar of a regular cigarette.[14] Tar is known to cause cancer. Marijuana also contains many of the other cancer-causing chemicals that are found in regular cigarettes.

Smoking marijuana can lead to many of the

People who begin using marijuana at an early age may be more likely to develop mental health disorders such as depression, suicidal thoughts, and schizophrenia.

ailments caused by smoking regular cigarettes. Those ailments include chronic bronchitis, frequent coughing, an overproduction of phlegm, and difficulty breathing.[15]

Marijuana also damages the body's cells and tissues that protect against diseases. The drug also can damage chromosomes. Users who become pregnant could have babies with learning difficulties. In older users, frequent marijuana use can lead to an increased risk of a heart attack.[16]

Marijuana by itself is harmful. Marijuana users build up a tolerance to the THC, and they need more of it to produce the same feeling. Eventually, they may turn to alcohol and other drugs to get high.[17]

Despite the dangers and the warnings, people continue to use marijuana. It has been estimated that more than fifteen million Americans are regular users of the drug. Also, every year, almost three million people try marijuana for the first time.[18]

As many as one in nine users may become addicted to marijuana.[19] Despite past perceptions, marijuana is, indeed, addictive. That means people cannot control their urge to use it.

"Some people definitely become psychologically dependent on it," said Brobson Lutz, a doctor in New Orleans. "They need it and miss it if they do not have it."[20]

In fact, the number of people who are dependent on marijuana is growing. One study found that the number of people who use marijuana has remained about the same as it was about ten years ago. However, the number of those who say they are dependent on marijuana has increased. Scientists believe the higher THC levels in today's marijuana may play a role in increased addictions to marijuana.[21] Marijuana is stronger, and users want to continue to feel that high.

Studies have shown that marijuana users who become dependent on the drug do not usually consume larger amounts of it. Instead, they tend to smoke more often, until they are high almost all the time.[22]

Mary Ellen Ruff is the senior case manager for programs at Inova Kellar Center. The center, in Fairfax, Virginia, offers substance-abuse programs for children. Ruff said many people still believe that marijuana is not addictive, "and many kids will try to use this as an argument to continue using it." However, it is addictive, she said. "And kids often report physical symptoms when they stop using marijuana. These might include headaches, irritability, sleep disturbance and cravings."[23]

"The danger is, kids don't think they can become dependent," said Teresa Latham. "But a lot of them become regular users before they even know it. Because they really have such a hard time giving it up, they would love to see people not get dependent on it."[24]

Billy Martin is a professor at Virginia Commonwealth University and a pharmacologist. A pharmacologist is an expert on the science of drugs. Martin has studied marijuana for many years. "Almost any drug that makes people feel good is going to produce dependence," he said. "I think it's become much clearer in the last five to ten years that marijuana does produce that dependence."[25]

Until recently, there were very few programs to deal with marijuana addiction. Now, however, there is hope. Before they can be helped, marijuana users need to realize they have a problem. Then, they need to want to do something about it.

CHAPTER FIVE

DOWN FROM THE HIGH

By all accounts, Adam, Brian, Charlie, and Danny (not their real names) have had tough lives. They all have at least one parent who has had a serious drug problem. But the background shared by these four boys cannot excuse the bad choices they made.

Adam was only in third grade when

he first tried marijuana. He became a regular user, and then he started selling it. When Adam moved from Arizona to Virginia, he continued his illegal ways.

Adam, by now in seventh grade, met with a supplier once a month. The supplier sold Adam marijuana. Adam divided the marijuana into little plastic bags. He brought the bags to school and gave out free samples to his classmates.

Some students tried it, and liked it. They began buying marijuana from Adam regularly. Charlie was one of Adam's frequent customers. Brian bought marijuana from Adam one time.[1]

Adam was busted when a brave student told the school security officer. Adam was suspended from school, and will probably be expelled. He was charged with possession with intent to distribute marijuana on school property, and distribution of marijuana on school property.[2] He may end up in a juvenile detention facility.

Adam told the security officer he sold marijuana to Brian and Charlie. The security officer first spoke with Brian. At first, Brian denied it. Officer Angela Hanby of the Prince William County Police was called to the school. She searched Brian. She found a bag of marijuana under the insole of his shoe.

The next morning, the security officer approached Charlie as he got off the school bus and started walking into school. Charlie did not have marijuana on him. But a video camera on the school bus recorded what had happened to it. On the bus that morning, Charlie asked Danny to hold a bag of marijuana for him. Charlie had heard he might be searched that day in school.

Danny stuck the marijuana in his pocket as a favor to his friend. Danny's involvement was not at the same level as Brian's or Charlie's, but he received the same punishment. All three boys were suspended from school and charged with drug possession. Charges may be dropped if

MYTH		FACT
Smoking marijuana is safer than smoking cigarettes.	VS.	Not true! Smoking marijuana is worse than smoking cigarettes. One joint affects the lungs as much as *four* cigarettes.

they complete a drug-awareness and treatment program.[3]

Buying marijuana is against the law. It is also against the law to use it. And selling marijuana is a very serious crime. "Distribution is certainly way more serious" than simple possession, said Jay Lanham, vice narcotics officer for Prince William County Police. "We're talking about the difference between a felony," which is a major crime with severe punishment, "and a misdemeanor," a minor crime with a lighter punishment. "Any distribution charge is a felony."[4]

Lanham also said, "Of course, then you start getting into other issues, such as violence, when you start selling it."[5]

Teresa Latham said students who "take the step [from using] to distribution either don't understand the potential for what they're putting themselves up for, or they're willing to take that risk."

"To me, that says a lot about what's going on with them," she said. "We really need to intervene. For someone who is to the point where they're willing to take that step to get whatever it is that they are using, their priorities are out of whack."[6]

Using marijuana can also lead kids to commit other crimes. Some kids end up stealing money so that they can pay for their marijuana habit. Adam sold his small bags of regular marijuana, or swag, for about twenty or thirty dollars a bag. The bags contained enough marijuana for about five joints. For someone with a regular marijuana habit, that amount does not last very long.

Marijuana leads to problems in school, too. The drug affects memory and recall. Teens who use marijuana have difficulty concentrating and remembering information. In fact, studies have found that students with a D average are four times more likely to have used marijuana than students with an A average. Also, teens who use marijuana are twice as likely as nonusers to drop out of school.[7]

"Studies show that heavy marijuana use impairs a teen's ability to concentrate and retain information," said Larry S. Fields, president of the American Academy of Family Physicians. "This is especially problematic during these peak learning and testing years."[8]

Weight gain can be one of many undesirable side effects.

Marijuana can even affect appearance. Regular users smell like smoke. Their eyes are red and glazed over. They also may gain a lot of weight. This is because marijuana increases the appetite. The slang term for getting hungry after getting high is "the munchies." Weight gain might be desirable for a few people, but it is undesirable for most.

Latham said that in her experiences, she has found that girls are just as likely as boys to try marijuana, but girls usually do not become heavy users because they are concerned about the weight gain.

The most recent National Survey on Drug Use and Health found that in 2002, 2003, and 2004, the number of teenaged girls who became first-time marijuana users exceeded the number of teenaged boys who tried it for the first time.[9]

"It's really sad the girls are winning," said Warren Seigel, a pediatrician at Coney Island Hospital in Brooklyn, New York. "This isn't the game they should be winning."[10]

Marijuana does not lead just to weight gain. It also causes users to do embarrassing things. People who are "stoned" may do or say things they normally would not. They might engage in risky sexual behavior. Also, getting busted in front of the entire school can be very embarrassing. That is what happened to an eighth-grade student in Massachusetts. He was suspected of dealing marijuana at Marshall Middle School. A police officer arrested the student at school and took him away in handcuffs.[11]

Using marijuana can also have consequences later in life. Many employers who work with the federal government require their workers to have a security clearance. To grant these clearances, employers investigate a potential worker's background. They interview friends, neighbors, and classmates. They ask about past drug use. They also may require drug tests.

Laura DiCesare is a public information officer in the Drug Enforcement Administration's (DEA) Washington, D.C., division. Every year, hundreds of college students ask her about internships. An internship is an unpaid position, but it offers valuable "real world" experience. DiCesare said that even though interns are not paid, they cannot work at the DEA if they do not pass a drug test. Many other employers, private and public,

Marijuana is harmless when you are a young user just having fun.

vs.

Marijuana can harm in many different ways, and kids can be affected more than adults. Using marijuana can lead to health, safety, social, learning, and behavioral problems.

require prospective interns or employees to undergo drug tests.

"What you do now will affect you later in your life," said Kevin Foley, assistant special agent in charge of the DEA's Washington, D.C. division. "Bad decisions can affect the rest of your life." He explained that many opportunities are denied to people who use marijuana. "These choices you thought you had, you might be eliminating" if you use the drug.

"No one's perfect. No one expects you to be perfect," Foley added. "But if you try to get through and stay on the right road, you'll keep most of your choices."[12]

Employers are not the only ones who test for drug use. Athletic organizations do, too. Several athletes have risked their careers over marijuana use. Ross Rebagliati of Canada won a gold medal for snowboarding in the 1998 Winter Olympics in Nagano, Japan. However, the medal was taken away a few days later after a post-race test found traces of marijuana in his system. Rebagliati said he had not smoked marijuana, but admitted that he had been to a party where people were using it. The medal was given back to him a few days after it was taken away because officials said the drug-testing policy regarding marijuana was not clear.[13]

The National Basketball Association (NBA) began testing players for marijuana use in 1999. Players knew what month they would be tested, but not the exact day. Nevertheless, "ten or twenty players . . . would test positive," said William Jacobs, a professor at the University of Florida who researches drug abuse. "That speaks of a problem with guys who couldn't stop long enough not to get caught."[14]

In the NBA, players who test positive for marijuana use must enter a drug-treatment program.

NBA players Damon Stoudamire (front) and Rasheed Wallace give a statement after both were cited for misdemeanor marijuana possession.

If they have a second positive test, they must pay a hefty fine. Players who have a third positive test may be suspended from playing.

The National Football League (NFL) also tests its players randomly for marijuana. Football players who test positive must enter a drug-treatment program. Subsequent positive tests lead to fines and suspensions.

Why would anyone use marijuana? It is important to remember that "everybody" is not doing it. About half of all American teenagers do not try marijuana before they graduate from high school. But unfortunately, some do try it. Some even become regular users.

Some people, like Adam, Brian, Charlie, and Danny, have parents or family members who are drug users. They are accustomed to drugs being around. They might also be more likely to use marijuana or become addicted to drugs because of their genetic makeup. Many experts believe that the trait to become addicted to a drug is inherited, much like eye color or height.

Others use marijuana because they have friends who use it, and they feel pressured to go along with the crowd. Some kids use marijuana to deal with feelings of anxiety, anger, depression, and even boredom.[15]

Karen (not her real name) first tried marijuana the summer before she started high school. She also started drinking. She had a family history of addiction and soon became addicted herself. She lost interest in her schoolwork and sports, and started lashing out at her parents.[16]

Drug counselor Theresa Latham said there is no picture of the "typical kid" who uses marijuana. "It can be the kid you would not expect, who has every intention of going to college, but tried marijuana for fun and got really hooked on it," she said. "I have also seen kids with intact families,

MYTH   FACT

It is safer to drive "stoned" than to drive drunk.

vs.

Drivers who are stoned react differently than drivers who are drunk. But both conditions are unsafe because in each case, the driver is impaired. Drivers should not drive under the influence of anything.

who got involved 'just because.' They can't give you a good reason."[17]

Sometimes, good people do make bad choices. They try marijuana. They become regular users. Their health suffers, and so does their future. They may even start taking other, even more dangerous, illegal drugs.

Timmen L. Cernak is a psychiatrist who specializes in treating people with addictions. He says that if people do not try marijuana until they are at least 18 years old, they still have a ten percent chance of becoming dependent on it. However,

MYTH		FACT
Marijuana is not addictive.	vs.	Recent research has shown that use of the drug can lead to dependence. Some users have developed withdrawal symptoms when they have not used marijuana for a period of time.

younger teens who try marijuana have a much greater chance of becoming addicted. Also, the addiction will occur quickly, and will cause much more disruption in their lives.[18]

There is hope, however. Every year, hundreds of thousands of people enter drug-treatment programs. Karen was one of those people. She, like the others who entered programs, wanted to kick the marijuana habit.

CHAPTER SIX

HELP AND HOPE

Karen started smoking marijuana the summer before she started ninth grade. She was lying to her parents, and sneaking out of the house at night to party.

Recognizing there was a serious problem, Karen's parents arranged for her to see a counselor. When Karen did not improve, her parents made a drastic decision: They sent her away for several months to a wilderness treatment program. There, sheltered from the influences and pressures of her regular life, and surrounded by young people who, like her, were trying to overcome addiction, Karen received the help she needed.[1]

In 2002, almost three hundred thousand people who entered drug treatment programs reported marijuana as the main drug they abused.[2] However, up until a few years ago, marijuana users had difficulty finding help. Few experts realized marijuana was addictive. Now, they understand that it is.

Many marijuana users also recognize that the drug is harmful. They realize that it is hurting them physically, emotionally, and even financially. However, they are unable to control their urge to continue using it.

Also, some people may not realize they are addicted until it is too late. "Kids develop their dependence faster," said Teresa Latham. "Five to 15 weeks is all that it takes—sometimes less."[3]

Younger people develop dependence faster because at that stage in their lives, their brains and their bodies are not yet fully developed, and all changes occur at a fast pace.[4]

The Inova Kellar Center is a leader in recognizing the need to offer programs for marijuana addiction. The center was established in 1992. It is located outside of Washington, D.C., in Fairfax, Virginia. It is the area's only not-for-profit mental health center.

The Kellar Center provides many programs, including substance abuse programs, to help teens and their families. The programs are geared to teens thirteen to eighteen years old. The average age of teens in the program is sixteen.

Each year, about one hundred teens come to the Kellar Center with drug problems. Of those one hundred, ninety come specifically for help with marijuana addiction. Mary Ellen Ruff is the senior case manager for Inova's programs. She said the number of teens seeking help has increased in the past three years. One reason is because marijuana has become more available.[5] Many kids become exposed to it so often that they finally give in to temptation, peer pressure, and curiosity and try it.

Ned (not his real name) is a teen who completed

Drug treatment centers, such as this WestCare facility in Kentucky, help people to recover from their drug dependency.

a Kellar Center program. Ned had never gotten into trouble with the law over his marijuana addiction. However, his parents caught him several times smoking marijuana. They pleaded with him to stop, but Ned either would not or could not.

By the time Ned came to the Kellar Center, he was smoking up to six times a day, from the time he woke up "to the last thing he did before going to bed," Ruff said.[6] Formerly an A-B student, Ned was now getting Ds. His eyes were constantly red, and his clothes smelled of marijuana smoke. He had become sneaky in his attempts to hide his illegal "stash" from his parents.

When Ned was first admitted to the program, he said he was just biding his time. He was convinced that as soon as he was able to leave the program, he would return to using marijuana. But through the course of treatment, Ned changed.

Like all program participants, Ned attended therapy sessions with other teens. "We do a lot of education on making lifestyle changes since it is so difficult for kids to make changes, especially when they're giving up something they really love," Ruff said.[7]

Ned also attended group therapy sessions. These sessions involved his family as well as other teens with their family members. Family involvement is very important to a teen's success in the program, Ruff said.[8]

Ned also was required to attend two meetings every week of Narcotics Anonymous (NA). This worldwide organization, which was established in the 1950s, is based on Alcoholics Anonymous. Membership is open to all drug addicts seeking a recovery process and a support network. Ned met the Kellar Center's requirement to find a sponsor in NA. The sponsor helped support Ned through his recovery.

Ned spent seven months in the Kellar Center program. Throughout his treatment, Ned was required to take random drug tests. He passed them all. He brought his grades up, graduated from high school, and enrolled in a local university. "At last report, he was doing well," Ruff said.[9]

So far, Ned is a success story. However, Ruff said that many people have a very difficult time ending their addiction.[10] Why is it so difficult? Some people find it hard because of peer pressure. They may need to establish a new circle of friends. Latham said it is important for youths to create "recovery networks," which are friends who do not use drugs.[11]

Some marijuana users have difficulty quitting because they cannot handle the withdrawal symptoms. Studies have shown that many marijuana users experience these symptoms. They are similar to the withdrawal symptoms

Talking to a favorite teacher or a group of friends can help a user on his or her path to recovery.

experienced by people who are trying to stop using cocaine or smoking tobacco cigarettes. The symptoms include anxiety, aggression, and irritability.[12]

Another reason it may be difficult to end marijuana addiction is because users are in denial. Denial is a false belief. Like Ned, many marijuana addicts do not truly believe they have a problem. They think "everyone" is using marijuana, and it is no big deal. Being in denial is part of the illness of drug addiction.

Sometimes, drug addicts are treated with medication. However, there is no medication to treat marijuana addiction. Scientists are learning more and more about THC and its effect on the body. Eventually, they may be able to develop a medicine that will block the effects of THC.

In the meantime, programs for marijuana addiction focus on counseling, education, and support systems. When teens are referred to Latham for drug use, she gathers a lot of information before recommending a course of treatment. Latham asks the teen how long he or she has been using marijuana, how often, and how much. She also asks about family and social issues, how the teen is doing in school, who the teen lives with, and whether the teen has previously tried to quit using.

Latham said that often, teens have difficulty overcoming their addiction because they use marijuana in combination with other drugs. "They're combining marijuana with whatever they can get their hands on—which is really dangerous."[13] For example, some teens take Ritalin tablets, which are prescribed for hyperactivity, and crush them. Then, they sprinkle the mixture on top of the marijuana. This practice is called "snowcapping."

After gathering information, Latham meets with a team of experts. The team may include a social worker, doctor, nurse, and psychiatrist. The team determines whether the teen needs treatment, and what kind of treatment. Latham said treatment is recommended for about ninety percent of the teens she sees. The remaining ten percent, she said, were probably caught the first time they brought marijuana to school, or the first time they used it. Latham may not recommend treatment for these teens, but she does ask them to stay in contact with her.

Teens who are recommended for treatment are assigned to a counselor or case manager. The counselor works with the teen and his or her family to develop a treatment plan. The plan lists problems, treatment goals, and the specific steps that will be taken to help the user overcome his or her addiction. Users will need to learn healthful ways to deal with stress, anger, social anxiety, or boredom.

Treatment options vary. Some teens continue in their regular school. However, they must attend weekly drug education programs in the evenings. Some teens also attend group or individual therapy sessions.

Another option is day treatment. Instead of attending their regular school, teens meet in special centers. Teachers help them with their school work in the mornings. Afternoons are devoted to drug education and therapy sessions. It is an intense program, but participants return home every night.

Outpatient programs are offered in health clinics, counselor's offices, hospitals and local health department offices, among other places. They require people to attend anywhere from nine to twenty hours of treatment activities every week.

Some teens in treatment have other problems such as attention deficit and hyperactivity disorder. The treatment plan includes help for these types of disorders, too, in order to improve the chances of recovery from the drug addiction.

An important part of the treatment plan is follow-up care. This occurs after a teen has successfully completed the program. The teen "checks in" occasionally with the counselor, to make sure everything is going well.

Many people who successfully complete a drug treatment program relapse. That is, they return to using drugs. The relapse may be temporary. It is important for the teen to get help right away, so that the relapse does not become permanent.

Overcoming marijuana addiction is hard work. It is not always a straight line to recovery. Timmen L. Cernak is a psychiatrist who specializes in treating people with addictions. He has seen many people relapse. But he also has seen many people recover. "I have . . . experienced the other side of the whirlpool of addiction—the side

MYTH   FACT

Marijuana makes you mellow.

VS.

This is not always the case. Research shows that kids who use marijuana are nearly four times more likely than non-users to report they have engaged in violent behavior.

where everyone emerges stronger than ever, more deeply in touch with themselves, and con- nected to one another more than ever, and healthier than ever," he said.[14]

Just ask Ned, Karen, and the thousands of oth- ers who overcome marijuana addiction: It is worth the struggle to reclaim a healthy life, and guarantee the opportunity for a bright future.

GLOSSARY

addictive—Causing compulsive need for and use of a harmful substance.

assessment—Official judgment of the importance, value, or significance of something.

conspiracy—Secret plan to accomplish a bad or illegal act.

decriminalize—To remove or reduce the criminal classification or status.

denial—False belief.

dependent—Need for something or someone.

felony—A serious crime that receives harsh punishment, such as a prison term of more than one year.

genetics—Branch of biology that deals with the heredity and variation of organisms.

hemp—Type of *cannabis sativa* plant with very low THC levels.

inhibit—To prohibit from doing something.

misdemeanor—Less serious crime.

pharmacology—Science of drugs.

phlegm—Mucus secreted in abnormal amounts in respiratory passages.

potent—Strong, powerful.

recreational—Relating to occasional or leisurely drug use.

treaty—Formal agreement between two or more nations.

withdrawal—Feelings of pain and discomfort that come from ending the use of an addictive drug.

CHAPTER NOTES

Chapter 1. Shots in the Night

1. Josh White, "Triggerman in Alleged Drug Hit to Testify: He's Expected to Say Ex-Friend Hired Him," *The Washington Post*, January 13, 2002, p. PW-1.
2. Josh White, "Greed Cited in Slaying Tied to Prince William Ring: Shooting Exposed Extensive Drug Cartel," *The Washington Post*, January 9, 2002, p. B-1.
3. Josh White, "In N.Va. Drug Ring, Good Kids Went Bad," *The Washington Post*, August 12, 2001, p. A-1.
4. Donna Leinwand, "Ecstasy drug trade turns violent: The rave culture's 'peace and love' pill bloodies the suburbs as dealers battle for turf and profits," *USA Today*, May 16, 2001, p. A-01.
5. White, "In N.Va. Drug Ring, Good Kids Went Bad," p. B-1.
6. Ibid.
7. Personal interview with Steve Straka, November 21, 2005.
8. Josh White, "Va. Drug Dealer Guilty of Murder for Hire: Prince William Jury To Decide Fate in Supplier's Slaying," *The Washington Post*, January 23, 2002, p. B-2.
9. Josh White, "Va. Man Testified About Killing Alleged Drug Dealer," *The Washington Post,* June 2, 2001, p. B-3.
10. White, "Triggerman in Alleged Drug Hit to Testify:

He's Expected to Say Ex-Friend Hired Him,"
p. PW-1.

11. Associated Press, "Spare Me, Killer Asks Jury,"
Richmond Times Dispatch, January 24, 2002, p. B-2.

12. Rob Seal, "Death row inmate talks,"
PotomacNews.com, September 25, 2005, <http://
www.potomacnews.com/servlet/Satellite?page-
name=WPN/MGArticle/WPN_BasicArticle&c=M
GArticle&cid=1031785265399> (May 11, 2006).

13. Personal interview with Kevin Foley, November 21,
2005.

14. Ibid.

15. Personal interview with Steve Straka.

16. Josh White, "Drug-Related Slaying Trial Believed
Just the Tip of Charges," *The Washington Post*,
January 6, 2002, p. C-1.

17. "InfoFacts: Marijuana," *National Institute on Drug
Abuse*, n.d., <www.drugabuse.gov/Infofacts/
marijuana.html> (October 31, 2005).

18. Associated Press, "Marijuana use levels in adults up
sharply," *Houston Chronicle*, May 5, 2004, p. A-10.

Chapter 2. A Powerful Plant

1. Personal interview with Angela Hanby, October 27,
2005.

2. Loma G. Davies Silcott, "Wily Weed," *Listen*,
Volume 58, Number 4, December 1, 2004, p. 12.

3. Joseph M. Rey, Andres Martin, Peter Krabman, "Is
the Party Over? Cannabis and juvenile psychiatric
disorders over the past 10 years," *Journal of the*

American Academy of Child and Adolescent Psychiatry, 2004, Volume 43, Issue 10, p. 1194.

4. Charles Elmore, "Opinions are equally divided when it comes to what penalties should be for athletes who use marijuana," *The Palm Beach Post*, May 23, 2004, p. B-1.

5. George Biernson, "The Harmful Effects of Marijuana," published in *Contemporary Issues Companion*, Louise I. Gerdes, editor (San Diego, California: Greenhaven Press, 2002), p. 17.

6. Personal interview with Teresa S. Latham, November 7, 2005.

7. Personal interview with Kevin Foley, November 21, 2005.

8. Personal interview with Angela Hanby, October 27, 2005.

9. Lester Picker, "Marijuana Prices and Use," n.d., <www.nber.org/digest/jw100/27703.html> (October 24, 2005).

10. Lee Green and Michael Josephson, "The Demonized Seed: As a recreational drug, industrial hemp packs the same wallop as zucchini. So why does the U.S. Drug Enforcement Agency continue to deny America this potent resource? Call it Reefer Madness," *The Los Angeles Times Magazine*, January 18, 2004, p. 12.

Chapter 3. An Ancient Crop

1. E.J. Turner, "Cannabis in History," *www.ephidrina. org*, 1998, <www.ephidrina.org/cannabis/history. html> (October 24, 2005).

2. "A Concise History of Marihuana, or A Cannabis Timeline," *parascope.com*, August 1997, <www.parascope.com/articles/0897/timeline.htm> (October 24, 2005).
3. Ibid.
4. Charles Whitebread, "The History of the Non-Medical Use of Drugs in the United States," *Speech to the California Judges Association's 1995 Annual Conference*, n.d., <www.druglibrary.org/schaffer/History/whiteb1.htm> (November 4, 2005).
5. Larry "Ratso" Sloman, *Reefer Madness: A History of Marijuana* (New York: St. Martin's Press, 1979), pp. 127-132.
6. "A Concise History of Marihuana."
7. "Single Convention on Narcotic Drugs: Regulation of Cannabis—Cultivation," *wikipedia.org*, n.d., <oen.wikipedia.org/wiki/Single_Convention_on_Narcotic_Drugs> (October 31, 2005).
8. Ibid.
9. "Kerry Edwards admitted drug use, Marijuana taints presidential bids," *The Washington Times*, February 22, 2004, p. A-1.
10. "InfoFacts: Marijuana," *National Institute on Drug Abuse*, n.d., <www.drugabuse.gov/Infofacts/marijuana.html> (October 31, 2005).
11. Ibid.
12. Elisabeth Fraser, "The Medical Marijuana Debate: An Overview," published in *Contemporary Issues Companion*, Louise I. Gerdes, editor (San Diego, California: Greenhaven Press, 2002), p. 85.
13. Daniel Costello, "Unorthodox uses for medicinal

marijuana: The drug is being recommended by some doctors for conditions such as depression and ADD," *Los Angeles Times*, February 23, 2004, Health Section, F-3.

14. Ibid.

15. Ed Vogel, "Voters unlikely to pass pot plan," *Las Vegas Review/Journal*, March 22, 2004, p. B-1.

16. Eric Schlosser, "Make Peace with Pot," *The New York Times*, April 26, 2004, p. A-19.

17. "Fact & Fiction: Marijuana is NOT Medicine," *Drug Enforcement Administration website*, n.d., <www.justthinktwice.com/factfiction/MarijuanaisMedicine.cfm> (September 24, 2005).

Chapter 4. Change in the Brain

1. Ronald G. Shafer, "Marijuana Addiction: One Family's Nightmare," published in *Contemporary Issues Companion*, Louise I. Gerdes, editor (San Diego, California: Greenhaven Press, 2002), pp. 117–121.

2. Ibid., p. 118.

3. Loma G. Davies Silcott, "Wily Weed," *Listen*, Volume 58, Number 4, December 1, 2004, p. 12.

4. *Suspect Your Teen is Using Drugs or Drinking: A Brief Guide to Action for Parents*, undated brochure published by the American Academy of Pediatrics and the National PTA.

5. Personal interview with Teresa S. Latham, November 7, 2005.

6. "Marijuana: Facts Parents Need to Know," *National Institute on Drug Abuse*, n.d., <www.

drugabuse.gov/MarijBroch/Marijparentstxt.html>
(September 24, 2005).

7. Personal interview with Teresa S. Latham.

8. Charles Elmore, "Opinions are equally divided when it comes to what penalties should be for athletes who use marijuana," *The Palm Beach Post*, May 23, 2004, p. B-1.

9. George Biernson, "The Harmful Effects of Marijuana," published in *Contemporary Issues Companion*, Louise I. Gerdes, editor (San Diego, California: Greenhaven Press, 2002), p. 17.

10. "Marijuana: Facts Parents Need to Know."

11. "Marijuana Use Affects Blood Flow in Brain Even After Abstinence," *American Academy of Neurology*, February 7, 2005, <http://www.aan.com/press/press/index.cfm?fuseaction=release.view&release=250> (May 11, 2006).

12. Biernson, p. 15.

13. Timmen L. Cernak, M.D., *Marijuana: What's a Parent to Believe?* (Center City, Minnesota: Hazeldon Press, 2003), p. 4.

14. "Tips for Teens: The Truth about Marijuana," *National Clearinghouse for Alcohol and Drug Information*, n.d., <http://ncadi.samhsa.gov> (September 24, 2005).

15. NewsRx.com and NewsRx.net, "Drug Abuse: Marijuana associated with same respiratory symptoms as tobacco," *Life Science Weekly*, February 1, 2005, p. 507.

16. Brobson Lutz, "Joint Session," *New Orleans Magazine*, September 1, 2005, p. 32.

17. Biernson.

18. Erik Goldman, "Teen drug experimentation rates same as in 1970s: conversion from initial use to addiction is most strongly influenced by the nature of the drug itself," *Internal Medicine News*, April 1, 2005.

19. Ibid.

20. Lutz.

21. United Press International, "Researchers Say Marijuana Addiction is Up," May 5, 2004.

22. Cernak, p. 46.

23. Personal interview with Mary Ellen Ruff, November 21, 2005.

24. Personal interview with Teresa S. Latham, November 7, 2005.

25. Tammie Smith, "Medical-Marijuana Advocates Meet: Researchers at Conference in Charlottesville are Talking about New Developments," *Richmond Times-Dispatch*, May 22, 2004, p. B-2.

Chapter 5. Down From the High

1. Personal interview with Angela Hanby, October 27, 2005.

2. Ibid.

3. Ibid.

4. Personal interview with Jay Lanham, October 27, 2005.

5. Ibid.

6. Personal interview with Teresa S. Latham, November 7, 2005.
7. "Marijuana use can threaten teen's academic successes," *PR Newswire*, October 4, 2005.
8. Ibid.
9. Ceci Connolly, "Teen Girls Using Pills, Smoking More Than Boys," *The Washington Post*, February 9, 2006, p. A-3.
10. Ibid.
11. Anand Vaishnav, "A Hard Lesson: Alarmed over Marijuana, A Principal Cracks Down," *Boston Globe*, April 22, 2004, p. B-1.
12. Personal interview with Kevin Foley, November 21, 2005.
13. Charles Elmore, "Opinions are equally divided when it comes to what penalties should be for athletes who use marijuana," *The Palm Beach Post*, May 23, 2004, p. B-1.
14. Ibid.
15. "InfoFacts: Marijuana," *National Institute on Drug Abuse*, n.d., <www.drugabuse.gov/Infofacts/marijuana.html> (October 31, 2005).
16. Timmen L. Cernak, M.D., *Marijuana: What's a Parent to Believe?* (Center City, Minnesota: Hazeldon Press, 2003), pp. 165–166.
17. Personal interview with Teresa S. Latham.
18. Cernak, p. 57.

Chapter 6. Help and Hope

1. Timmen L. Cernak, M.D., *Marijuana: What's a*

CHAPTER NOTES

Parent to Believe? (Center City, Minnesota: Hazeldon Press, 2003), pp. 166–167.

2. Marijuana: Facts for Teens," *National Institute on Drug Abuse*, n.d., <www.nida.nih.gov/MarijBroch/Marijteenstxt.html> (October 31, 2005).
3. Personal interview with Teresa S. Latham, November 7, 2005.
4. Cernak, p. 48.
5. Personal interview with Mary Ellen Ruff, November 21, 2005.
6. Ibid.
7. Ibid.
8. Ibid.
9. Ibid.
10. Ibid.
11. Personal interview with Teresa S. Latham.
12. "University of Vermont: Marijuana withdrawal reported by teens seeking treatment," May 10, 2005, <http://www.medicalnewstoday.com/medicalnews.php?newsid=24083> (May 11, 2006).
13. Personal interview with Teresa S. Latham.
14. Cernak, p. 4.

FURTHER READING

Books

Graves, Bonnie. *Drug Use and Abuse*. Mankato, Minn.: LifeMatters, 2000.

Hasday, Judy L. *Marijuana*. Philadelphia, Penn.: Chelsea House Publishers, 2000.

Hyde, Margaret O. *Drugs 101: An Overview for Teens*. Brookfield, Conn.: Twenty-First Century Books, 2003.

Laliberte, Michelle. *Marijuana*. Berkeley Heights, N.J.: MyReportLinks.com Books, 2005.

Internet Addresses

freevibe.com
 <http://www.freevibe.com>
  Read more about drugs and read about other teens' experiences with drugs or how they stayed away them.

NIDA for Teens
 <http://teens.drugabuse.gov>
  This site from the National Institute on Drug Abuse (NIDA) is full of information about marijuana and other drugs.

INDEX